HOOSIC RIVER

A poem

by David Crews

Published by NatureCulture®
NatureCulture Web Imprint
Northfield, Massachusetts

This Hoosic River *poem cycle is dedicated to the Hoosic River Watershed Association (hoorwa.org), a nonprofit citizen group that looks after the river. These poems were written while visiting various public-protected lands inside the river's watershed, places that reside in and around ancestral lands and the home today of Muhheaconneok and western Abenaki peoples. The river's name belongs to the Algonquin language family and Algonquin peoples came to this land as home over twelve thousand years ago as the last glaciers retreated from the region when the river too came into being.*

It is just as incongruous to place an Indian prairie name among our mountains as it was to plant the names of Pompey, Cicero and Virgil in central New York. Onondaga is not appropriate on our western plains.

– William Martin Beauchamp
Aboriginal place names of New York
1907

When Mojaves say the word for tears, *we return to our word for* river, *as if our river were flowing from our eyes.* A great weeping *is how you might translate it.* Or a river of grief.

– Natalie Diaz
Postcolonial Love Poem
2020

HOOSIC RIVER

North corridor

Carry it
like the river, she says

I leave the back door
walk up the rise
farmfield's west end
close the gate
follow the coyote's path
into the woods
to the pine grove
where huge White pines
      loom
into a canopy

just beyond
a slow descent
to a mountain stream
its flute, cross it
rocks mineral gray
piled and scattered
      slate, schist
into a mountain

into soft tufts
of Peat moss
Broom and Log moss
rock draped, fern
covered, fallen trees

At the summit
of West mountain
        2401 feet
above the level of the sea
just south of Spruce peak
Grass mountain
the northern Taconics
western rim
of what some call
the Vermont valley

here, the watershed's
ecotone
             a turn
from the compass rose
I open the map

feel its textures
where contours
         fall
in crevasse, moraine
recall the power
of glacial striation

to know how mountains
are sculpted, formed
from rock and cavern
water flows
springs in the forest
that rise through
limestoned earth
          here, land
of Chestnut-sided warblers
and no more chestnuts

I am a river
I once was a river

the rushing
of Little White creek
fades, comes closer
as I move toward
source, spring
the water flowing
over the falls
on beds of moss
deepened stones, soaks
into and down
the creek perhaps little
it will grow
          increasing
the more it falls away
the more it fills

on its way to the sea

Some of the forest
has been logged
          most of it
these trees
not old growth

who has touched
more of the land
we, or the river

and do the redstarts
know, do the ovenbirds
                    know

will the deep woods
remain broken
draped in oak limbs
          strewn about
Turkey tails climbing
Shaggy manes
in the lower haunts

how the wind
and rain shape
          the forest
for the songs
of Black-throated

blues, greens
Winter wrens and vireos
the thrushes collecting
how many
      are left

The river's water
twists and turns
down farmfields
under roads
the feeding streams
given away
by meandering groves
      of trees

collecting fertilizer
and feed
cow manure, pesticides
tractor oil and piss
fetored and pooling
      briefly
to descend
homemade rock
      dams
   as it drops
to the Walloomsac
where fly fishermen
scatter the slower waters
     under

rusted out bridges
freight train crossings
recycling centers
waterwaste treatment plants
warehouses ruined

at Hoosick falls
the water flows north
past abandoned
            factories
mills, ghost mills
lost concrete structures
along the river
before the last push
into the locks
of the Hudson

Locals speak
of a spot
            where
back in the 70s
the land was mined
for gravel
before protests
shut the company
                    down
Moses farm
the land now
        called

at the terminus
of the Owl kill

a confluence
where rivers

        gather

and stories say
once was an intertribal
meeting place
at the meeting
of the waters
Haudenosaunee

      Abenakis
Muhheaconneok
Hoosic, beyond place
      of stones

what does the river
know

East corridor

Deep in the Glastenbury
      wilderness
feeding streams

to the Walloomsac
network like veins
or synapse fire
from the source
the roots of great
Red oak
or what I imagine
them to be

my trust
          only goes
to certain depths
the map tells me

an unidentified bird
song throws tight
          little spirals
into far reaches
of hemlock forest
more a product
of an ecosystem
than a poem
so close to the edge
          of truth
and beauty

and to move north
alongside the AT ridge
in late May

is to be
chasing warblers
at the tail end
of mud season, moss
season
I step from rock
          to rock
a whisper in the woods
                    so light
streams flute away
to their
circadian rhythms

On the trail
to Bald mountain
a sitting rock
at the meeting point
of deciduous, conifer
forests
a meditation spot
on eco
          tones and life

there, miles ago
when I truly felt alone
before this chorus
of rattle, scree and jive
sweet
          sweet zoo

Blackburnian, Pine
Myrtle
the flies thick
and heavy in feel

They are dying
a friend once said to me
you know each year
there are fewer
and fewer
they don't come back

here, at the highest point
                around
is to visit too
with ravens

their calls
will alert bedrock
the West Ridge trail
to the firetower
on Glastenbury
chart the high elevations
                    that scape
the eastern boundary
of the watershed
            and even
in late spring
it already feels dry

and these birds
these trees

what will happen
to the rivers
       we know

Corridor

I hear the words
over
       and over again

Blessed is the human

whose strength
is in you, whose heart
is set
      on pilgrimage

     I will
bear myself fully
to each new moment
without regret
or hesitation

(this
         is a lie)

the river keeps time
as it moves
                  into space

the water
a broken mirror

the violence
         downstream

how does the river
talk
         what to say

will it always be
the deep song
         of pain

weeping, my friend
says

Is it only love
that makes a place

how does one carry
these depths

small calls of birds
on the ridge

the river carries
                    all of it

            will I
find myself
able to love

the way a river
            moves

between flute
and tense abandon

to be water
flowing over rock
through earth

            to be water
and not dream
of death

species lost
            thrushes, ash
            trees

to not live a life
of constant peril

wildfire, flood
riot
      gun

~~⌒~~

Central corridor, West

Southbound
from the northern
terminus
of the Taconic Crest
      trail

a hard climb
from route 346
where the Hoosic
snakes a way
through range
      and quarry
past state lines

how water
needs never
to think like this

what will
become of me

who, of those
        I love
will die

the only truth
        worth telling

Good thing
my pack's full
for this side
of the solstice
high on the ridge
one finds little water
alert, air quality again
not good

        and far
from the road
the birds know
                nothing
of distant wildfires
in Canada
the jet stream
filtering through
songs full of life

an aliveness
all around me

and the river
a quiet funnel
furrowed and rolling
          continually
over itself

from source
          to mouth
as it collects
                    gathers
          swells

the Veery knows rain
          song like
water draining
deep in the woods

in the music
I hear a longing

that reminds me
of these
          walking rhythms
my feet again
                    under me

I imagine
the dripping canopy
soaked duff
        leaf litter
the ferns heavy

if the warblers
would have me

East corridor

One squawk
beyond evergreen

and I know the being

        hello, I say
as if my words too

could catch
                the wind

Central corridor, East

Again,
      I am
lured to
the Appalachian trail

      up Sherman
brook

the rush
of water falls
over great rocks

drops and turns
      and falls

this old footpath

      haunt
of the mink
Oyster mushrooms
trailing tall trees
      forever
green, a high
thick canopy

ferns ferns
                    ferns

what does it all
mean

lone traveler
and your
ten thousand questions

3.8 miles
through mud
and hemlock
around glacial erratics

to East mountain
the Vermont border

You are traveling through

        the homelands
of the Mohican people

2340 feet
above the level
        of the sea

life and language
even here

Muhheaconneok,
      I say to myself

      as if
everything is not
already past

how would I ever
know
      a homeland

when I walk
this trail
I long to journey

and never do

        ⌒⊃

    North corridor

She was not
the forest

she was not
      the big trees
old canopy trees

or the distant stream
and its flute

she was not thick
                dark earth
        and dirt

she came
from deep forest

but the forest
was also in her

                a figure
among the ferns
who would visit

when sleep
        some nights

lifted
into cold wet
        air

I have come
                so far

and still

know so little
of this living world

If you love your love
love her thoughts
                    as well

are there enough
trees
for the forest
to hold me
            in fir
and hemlock

distant quiet
of secret bog
sphagnous root
and newt

I could sleep
                    here
feel deep
pools of breath
fill my chest

has she
            always been

have I

found her
        again

and how many times
will we fall
in love

with the broken
            beauty

of this dying
grief strickened
        world

⌒

South corridor

For fifteen hundred miles
the Appalachian trail
twists and turns
climbs and descends
        vista and ridge
again and again
northbound
till it finally crosses
the South branch
        of the Hoosic

as the river leaves
source waters
of what once was
Hoosac lake
now Cheshire reservoir
in Berkshire county
Massachusetts

The footpath
meanders around
field and pasture
before climbing
the south shoulder
      of Greylock
passing between
Cole mountain
Jones nose
over Saddle Ball mountain
to a summit 3491 feet
above sea level
(highest point
in the state)

Grey Lock
      Wawanolewat
was a western Abenakis
warrior and chieftain
from the Woronoke band
of Westfield river

who fought
for the Missisquoi
      Wabanaki coalition
and who led
resistance
against English armies
in the early
eighteenth century
conducting raids
on colonial settlements
from coastal Maine
along the Kennebec
      throughout
the Connecticut
river valley
to lake Champlain

as quickly
he would descend
upon guard and fort
he and his war parties
mobile
      and invisible
would again
disappear
into vast wilderness
of Green
mountain forest

In 1722
governor Samuel Shute
declared war
on the Maine Abenakis
                 proclaiming
the confederates
were robbers, traitors
and enemies
to his majesty
king George

and for the next
five years
ignoring calls
          and talks
for peace
from governors
in Albany
and New Hampshire
Grey Lock
continued a campaign
to liberate
Abenakis peoples

He was never
captured
          or killed
and his people
were not liberated

but fled
like so many
to Canada
and Grey Lock

       Wawanolewat
during the years
of peace that followed
fathered a daughter
      and a son
and with his family
carried out his days
to an old age
in the mountains
and rivers
     of his
ancestral homelands

and what happened
to him
no one really knows
and to speak
     of him
is to not let
his spirit rest

and to speak of him
an act of praise
praise the heart

and what
it carries
incessant longing

praise the river
        let me
come to the river

that falls
as water does
in time and rhythm
and what
of remembering

⟳

West corridor

Just before
Lock 3

the Hoosic
            bends

in light rain
wide and flat and shallow

more a flood plain
than a river

around Knicker
          bocker road
where the building
of new homes
clears broad space
among
                    river trees
trees that cover
blackbirds
          and grackles
catbirds
perched eagles

Down
          the road
a golf course
with meticulously
manicured greens
and fairways
sprawls above
houses

along the Hudson
now
          a canal
with docks

and touring boats
tied up
swimming rafts, out
in still water

I would have
        never
imagined
people would swim
in a canal

miles up
        river
before
the emptying
of Tomhannock
                creek

The sparrow
calls to me
        I am the sea
here, here
                here

in Schaghticoke
        the Hoosic
jettisons over a dam
where once

the water must have
                dropped
in dramatic
        falls

spilling unfettered
from the hanging
                cover
of the Taconic
mountains

⁓◦

Corridor

Why do I keep
writing
                of love

like it matters
enough

to heal anyone's real
wounds

as if grief didn't stem
every breath

as if pain
did not always fall
                down

I resent
the neat simplicity
        of it all

what does a river
know

about love

⁓◠

East corridor

        Leaves
have once again
fallen
from deciduous trees
into the season
of evergreen
and bedrock

the geometries
of mountains again
scape the land

my only connection
it sometimes feels

to a history
much larger than me

the self persists
        like a dying star

                  gone
and suddenly I see
clouds and light
feel the quiet
that comes
in the waiting
of winter

Nearly twenty
miles south
the Greylock
        massif
covered in crevice
krummholz of Balsam fir
and gnarled Red
spruce
        descends
to Sugar maple
Yellow birch

                    beech
at lower elevations
on north and east
facing slopes

oaks, hickories
to the south and west

I can see the trail
through valley
            and fen
forests of hemlock
and the soft
            branches
of White pine

traversing ridgeline
saddle
            and summit
ice crystals forming
at the edge of mud pack
now freezing

and I long
in the trembling
weight
            of it all

trail and mud and tree

and the feeling
that to walk
    this path
returns me to a source
I yet know of
that will find me

humbled, broken
    open

North corridor

It's cold

    so cold

it feels
uncommon these winters

but today
the snow is light
    as air

and the micro
    spikes
barely catch

and I can feel rocks
scraping, where mosses
incubate

and just to be
        here
causing harm
to the forest

and still
        I go

out from a tree
trunk, tracks
two by
        two
line
for a tail, mouse

and the Red
        squirrel
down a tree
a brief
        moment
a few leaps
up another
just over there

I climb

looking for
the smoothest
      route up

follow the prints
of wild dogs
for they know
the path
      of least
resistance

and mustelids
who must shape
these flumes
through and
      down
the rocks
of the hillside

I traverse
the summit ridge
sliding my feet
once in a while
into the watershed

for all the snow
here and down
on this side
of the mountain

will melt
and run there

as it always
      does

           ⌒○

West corridor

River for
ever new

a bright merganser
           holds
      then drifts

current borne

           ⌒○

Corridor

It began
when continents
           collided

four, five hundred

million years ago

     a return
water and earth

     All the while
time braided itself
into your verdigris flow

what does this say
about strength

I will give myself
to the boots'
walking rhythms
to deep woods

carved rock
from the last
         ice age

for what is here
     now
was also here
long ago

quartzite, schist
limestone
     sandstone

with slate layers
phyllite schist

from the Greek
      to split

plucked
in the glacial mass

down gorge
      and ravine

there is an edge
to everything

Appalachian
Taconic, Green
      Hoosac

in a series
of uplifts
the peneplain
      formed

      Nothing
in the world
is as soft
and yielding as water

put foot to rock
I tell myself
before dirt

a history that began
inside a permanent
body of snow

and interlocking
                    crystals
of mineral ice
how it pressed
upon land
          and scape

cirques
of the shaped valleys

in wedging
abrasion, plucking

freeze
          and expansion
to fractured rock
and glacial
          retreat

where striation
stripped bedrock

how water
works its way
into joint
      and crack

to split and freeze
and split

for most
Northeast rivers
run south
      and east
to the sea

            Yet

for dissolving
the hard
      and inflexible

bring me
to filling pools
      falling
in fern covered
           eddies
peatland fens

let me wash
the dried mud

from my tired legs

          cup
cold clear water
wet my face

                    bathe
in warm sun

like one
who knows
          of pain

the words
elude me

I say
          it,
          the river
nurtures life

and I will
give myself

to the trees
to the ferns
the birds
          and moss
clad stones

stand
      in a beyond
      place

before time
and I am
      breathing

and we are
         alive

ACKNOWLEDGMENTS

Epigraphs from *Aboriginal place names of New York* by William Martin Beauchamp (1907) and *Postcolonial Love Poem* by Natalie Diaz (2020).

Italicized lines in order from: *Psalms*, translated by Thomas Nelson (1982, my change to human) and *In a Time of Violence* by Eavan Boland (1994) in "Corridor"; *Moordener Kill* by Paul Genega (2020) in "Central corridor, West"; *The Lightness Which Is Our World Seen from Afar* by Ven Begamudré (2006) in "North corridor"; *Strange to Explain* by Woods (2020) in "West corridor"; *The Far Field: Last Poems* by Theodore Roethke (1964) in "East corridor"; *One River, a Thousand Voices* by Claudia Castro Luna (2019) and *Tao Te Ching* by Lao Tzu, translated by Stephen Mitchell (1988) in "Corridor." See also, "Dispatches from the Beyond Place: Tales of the Hoosic River" by Lauren R. Stevens, with John Case & Wendy Hopkins, published by the Hoosic River Watershed Association (2017).

"North Corridor" was created in collaboration with percussionist, Daniel O'Connor, for HooRWA's "Music and Poetry Along the River." A reading of "East Corridor" and "South Corridor" were both recorded and published on North Country Public Radio. A cycle of six poems was performed at Byte in Hoosick Falls (NY) on the 15th of September 2023, a poetry + percussion improvisation with Daniel O'Connor.

Dear gratitude to Lis McLoughlin for all the care and work that went into this book. To Darryl McGrath for believing in the vision and heart. And to these careful readers: Paul Genega, Jenny Wong, Laura Waterman, Daniel O'Connor, Basia Wilson, and Piper Campbell. You help carry these poems (and me).

ABOUT THE AUTHOR

Originally from the state of New Jersey, where he served for fifteen years as a public high school literature teacher, David Crews now lives and works at Clear Brook farm, an organic fruit and vegetable farm located at the edge of the Hoosic river watershed in the Vermont valley, ancestral land of Muhheaconneok and western Abenaki peoples.

He cares for work that explores land and place, wild(er)ness, preservation, nonviolence, and serves as board member with the Waterman Fund. He received an MFA in Poetry from Drew University, where he studied with poet-artists Ross Gay, Aracelis Girmay, Ira Sadoff, and Judith Vollmer.

His books include *Incantation*, a limited edition handmade chapbook of poems designed and produced by Josh Dannin of Directangle Press (2022), *Wander-Thrush: Lyric Essays of the Adirondacks* (Ra Press, 2018), and *High Peaks* (Ra Press, 2015)—a poetry collection that catalogs hiking the "Adirondack 46ers" in upstate New York. Find David and his work at davidcrews*poetry*.com.

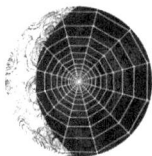

NatureCulture® Web

The mission of NatureCulture® is to help humans be in right relationship with the rest of the natural world. NatureCulture Web is our new imprint for books brought to us by like-minded authors and organizations.

www.nature-culture.net

Other NatureCulture® Books

2025

Dark Matter: Women Witnessing, Dreams Before Extinction, eds. Weil, et al
The Nemo Poems: A Martian Perspective, by Rodger Martin
The Sleeping Dogs of Lubec, by Rodger Martin
Writing the Land: The Rensselaer Plateau, NY
Writing the Land: Horizons
On Resilience: Morgan, Senechal & Writing the Land Poets
Handfast, Poems by Katherine Hagopian Berry
Montréal Undecided, by L. McLoughlin
Alex the Guard Shark, by L. McLoughlin
Alex, La Tuburona Guardiana, by L. McLoughlin

2024

The Black River: Death Poems
ed. Deirdre Pulgram-Arthen
Cayman Brac From Bluff to Sea
Writing the Land: The Connecticut River
Writing the Land: Wanderings I
Writing the Land: Wanderings II
Writing the Land: Virginia
Wriring the Land: Maine II, A Gathering
Writing the Land: Northeast, 2nd edition

2023

Writing the Land: Youth Write the Land
Writing the Land: Currents
Writing the Land: Channels
Writing the Land: Streamlines
Migrations and Home: The Elements of Place, ed.
Simon Wilson
From Root to Seed: Black, Brown, and Indigenous
Poets Write the Northeast, ed. Samaa Abdurraqib

2022

Writing the Land: Foodways and Social Justice
Writing the Land: Windblown I
Writing the Land: Windblown II
Writing the Land: Maine
LandTrust, poems by Katherine Hagopian Berry

Forthcoming (2026-2027)

Writing the Land: The Cayman Islands
Writing the Land: Pathways
Writing the Land: The Great Forest of Aughty
Writing the Land: Doolin, Ireland
Writing the Land: The First Five Years

www.ingramcontent.com/pod-product-compliance
Lightning Source LLC
Chambersburg PA
CBHW052026030426
42335CB00026B/3298